Baby Steps to Divine Destiny

by

Vickie Bryan

Copyright 2014

All rights reserved. No part of this publication may be reproduced without the prior permission of the publisher.

This book is protected by United States copyright laws.

Scripture reference in this book are taken from THE HOLY BIBLE, NEW INTERNATIONAL VERSION®, NIV® Copyright © 1973, 1978, 1984, 2011 by Biblica, Inc.™ Used by permission. All rights reserved worldwide.

Scripture reference in this book marked (NASB) are taken from THE HOLY BIBLE, New American Standard Bible®, Copyright © 1960, 1962, 1963,
1968, 1971, 1972, 1973, 1975, 1977, 1995 by The Lockman Foundation Used by permission." (www.Lockman.org)

Scripture quotations marked "KJV" are taken from the Holy Bible, King James Version, Cambridge, 1769.

Scripture quotations taken from the Scripture quotations marked (NLT) are taken from the Holy Bible, New Living Translation, copyright © 1996, 2004, 2007 by Tyndale House Foundation. Used by permission of Tyndale House Publishers, Inc., Carol Stream, Illinois 60188. All rights reserved.

V Ly Publishing LLC
Christian Imprint Books
1046 Church Rd, W 106-224
Southaven, MS 38671

ISBN: 978-0-9886814-8-4

Why Baby Steps

Baby Steps to Divine Destiny is written for those who desire to fulfill their God given destiny. Some people seem to thrive in their lives, but deep inside something is missing. Others find themselves struggling to make progress, dealing with the same old ruts time and time again. Some succeed in one area but strive in another. We do not have to continue on this hamster wheel. The purpose of *Baby Steps to Divine Destiny* is to let readers know there is a divine purpose for their lives. God is faithful. He made His plan known throughout the Bible to people just like you and me. May readers be inspired to step out one baby step at a time to discover their own divine destiny.

> *Direct my footsteps according to your word; let no sin rule over me. Psalm 119:123*

CONTENTS

Why Baby Steps.. v
God's Plans - A Hope and a Future 1
Baby Steps-Motivated to Succeed.......................... 3
What Plans?... 5
God's Plan Involves Man 7
Adam... 9
Moses 13
John the Baptist 31
Baby Step 1 - You Must Be Born Again............... 39
Why We Must Be Born Again 41
Restoration Back To God 43
Baby Steps to be Born Again 49
Baby Step Prayer for Salvation 51
Baby Steps for Backsliders.................................. 53
Baby Step Prayer for Backsliders 55
Baby Step 2 - Water Baptism 57
Baby Step Baptized in the Holy Spirit 69
Baby Step 3 - Be Filled with the Holy Spirit.......... 73
Just Do It - Take a Baby Step.............................. 85

God's Plans - A Hope and a Future

"For I know the plans I have for you," declares the Lord, "plans to prosper you and not to harm you, plans to give you hope and a future." Jeremiah 29:11 NIV

God has plans for you, and if you never walk with him, these plans may never be understood. I would say most people do not know what God has for them. They can find out, but for the most part, they do not know. When growing up, knowing God's plan was not how I was taught to address the future. My future was to be determined by what I would like to do or even more exact, what pays the most money for my ability. Maturing as a Christian, I truly wanted to know God's purpose for my life. I wanted to hear him say one day, *"Well done my good and faithful servant" (Matthew 25:21).*

In order to be found faithful, I needed to understand what the Lord had in mind for my life. Not only did he have a plan for me, but he knew about it before I was conceived.

""I knew you before I formed you in your mother's womb. Before you were born I let you apart and appointed you as my prophet to the nations." Jeremiah 1:5 NLT

Be encouraged. God knows you and is prepared to take you on a journey to discover your destiny, one baby step at a time.

Baby Steps-Motivated to Succeed

Oh, what an achievement, learning how to walk. Parents know it's coming, so they watch for the signs their toddler will soon be mobile. For a baby to take a first step, stages in his or her life must occur.

An infant grows physically and mentally from a newborn to a toddler. In this process he will roll over, crawl, scoot, and begin to pull up on anything within reach. Each one of these events will help achieve the goal of walking, just like mom and dad. With the aid of a parent's hand or even a finger, the baby gains stability and confidence to begin walking on his or her own two feet. At the toddler stage, the baby is ready to move around and begin the process of learning how to walk. Everybody has to take steps in order to accomplish any goal or aspiration in life.

When you decide to get out of bed in the morning, it takes a decision. For whatever reason, it's time to get up. First, you pull the covers off and put your feet on the floor. Next, you add your body weight and get up. Goal accomplished.

Serving the Lord and desiring to fulfill your divine destiny is a lofty goal. This goal with the necessary steps is already in the mind of God. It is the Lord who reveals his plan and destiny to his children. But the steps need to be understood. Just like frying an egg, driving a car, or cooking a meal, there are steps to take to accomplish the task. Sometimes smaller steps within steps are needed to accomplish the goal. For example, in preparing a meal each item on the menu will require different steps to achieve the one goal of making a meal. Similarly when serving God, one step leads to another to accomplish the big picture of divine purpose in a life. In whatever stage of life the reader maybe, fulfilling the purpose for which you were conceived can begin today, so let's get started.

What Plans?

In him we were also chosen, having been predestined according to the plan of him who works out everything in conformity with the purpose of his will. Ephesians 1:11 NIV

We need to understand God knows each of us. He knew our personality and His purpose for our lives before our conception. I never knew anything about the plans God had for me before being born again in Christ Jesus. I knew I wanted to be married and be a mom, but that was about it. When I accepted the Lord, this changed. The gifting of God began to show up in my life. I had an insatiable hunger to know God. I desired to serve him, to teach and preach his word. This was such a sharp contrast to the previous direction my life had taken. Truly, old things had passed away, and all things had become brand new for me (2 Corinthians 5:17). Prior to walking with the Lord, I knew absolutely nothing about what I just told you, absolutely nothing. So when I say, you must be born again to gain access to the plans of God for your life, I am a living example of this.

Therefore if anyone is in Christ, he is a new creature; the old things passed away; behold, new things have come. 2 Corinthians5:17 NIV

.

God's Plan Involves Man

In the Book of Genesis, one can read how God created our heavens and earth. The Word of God and the Spirit of God joined together to bring about God's plan of creation.

> *1In the beginning God created the heavens and the earth. 2Now the earth was formless and empty, darkness was over the surface of the deep, and the Spirit of God was hovering over the waters. 3And God said, "Let there be light," and there was light. Genesis 1:1-5 NIV*

The Spirit of God was right there waiting to create the spoken Word of God. Once the Word was released, the power of the Holy Spirit went to work and brought forth light. This is a snapshot of how God creates. Notice, God does not doubt his ability to accomplish his Word.

God created earth with man in mind. When God created mankind he made them responsible for certain tasks to be done in their lifetime. When he needs something done on earth, he looks for a person to work with him to accomplish his will. Since mankind's creation came in the image of God, they are highly capable of fulfilling their God given assignments.

> *So God created mankind in his own image, in the image of God he created them; male and female he created them. Genesis 1:27*

Adam

When earth became habitable, God formed one man and later his wife. Mankind was created in the image of God *"to rule over the fish in the sea and the birds in the sky, over the livestock and all the wild animals, and over all the creatures that move along the ground" (Genesis 1:26-27).*

> *4This is the account of the heavens and the earth when they were created, when the Lord God made the earth and the heavens. 5Now no shrub had yet appeared on the earth and no plant had yet sprung up, for the Lord God had not sent rain on the earth and there was no one to work the ground, 6but streams came up from the earth and watered the whole surface of the ground. 7Then the Lord God formed a man from the dust of the ground and breathed into his nostrils the breath of life, and the man became a living being. 15The Lord God took the man and put him in the Garden of Eden to work it and take care of it. Genesis 2:5-7,15*

Earth had no one to work the ground, so God formed a man. Adam was this man, and he walked with God. Think about it, it was just God and Adam. No other human existed anywhere. Imagine the closeness Adam enjoyed with his Creator. Not until after Adam named the living creatures did God create Adam's wife. So it is no telling how long

Adam walked in such an intimate relationship with God.

In these scriptures we can see Adam's life came with divine destiny prepared in advance for him. In Genesis 2:5 there was work to be done on earth, and no man to do it. So as apart of Adam's destiny, he got the job. In God's plan, he created mankind with specific assignments and various responsibilities. Adam served God as he worked the land and watched over the Garden of Eden.

> *19Now the Lord God had formed out of the ground all the wild animals and all the birds in the sky. He brought them to the man to see what he would name them; and whatever the man called each living creature, that was its name. 20So the man gave names to all the livestock, the birds in the sky and all the wild animals. Genesis 2:19-20*

As the first man created by God, Adam was a man of the earth, highly involved with God and his creation. Naming the animals fit Adam's aptitude and ability perfectly. God brought the different species of living creatures to Adam to "see" what he would name them. Whatever he decided to name the creature became its name. We notice Adam had the freedom to carry out his assignments according to his ability. In fulfilling divine purpose, God has a part and each person has his or her part. People must follow God's word of direction to them to fulfill their specific destiny. How do you know God's specific direction or command? The same way Adam did. God reveals his plan to those he calls. Those he calls must hear, understand, and believe the Word of God concerning their destiny. Speak it forth as God spoke forth creation. The word spoken releases faith in one's heart for God's plan. Whatever a person's divine destiny maybe, God will direct the path of those who will walk with him and fulfill their destiny.

> *Direct my footsteps according to your word; let no sin rule over me.*
> *Psalms 110:133*

Moses

The Lord will use circumstances throughout a person's life to prepare them for his purposes. Moses becomes our next Biblical figure to reveal the workings of God in fulfillment of divine destiny.

Without the faith of Moses' family, he would have died. At the time of his birth, the king of Egypt had issued an edict to kill all male babies born to an Israelite. The martyr Stephen spoke of these events before he was stoned to death as written in the Book of Acts.

> *6God spoke to him (Abraham)* in this way: 'For four hundred years your descendants will be strangers in a country not their own, and they will be enslaved and mistreated. 7But I will punish the nation they serve as slaves,' God said, 'and afterward they will come out of that country and worship me in this place.'17"As the time drew near for God to fulfill his promise to Abraham, the number of our people in Egypt had greatly increased.*
>
> *18Then'a new king, to whom Joseph meant nothing, came to power in Egypt.' 19He dealt treacherously with our people and oppressed our ancestors by forcing them to throw out their newborn babies so that they would die. 20"At that time Moses was born, and he was no*

> *ordinary child. For three months he was cared for by his family. 21When he was placed outside, Pharaoh's daughter took him and brought him up as her own son. 22Moses was educated in all the wisdom of the Egyptians and was powerful in speech and action. Acts 7:6-7;17-22 NIV *my addition*

Moses not only survived the edict of the king, he was reared as a member of Pharaoh's own household. Circumstances at the time of Moses' birth were beyond his control. Nevertheless, God used these events to prepare Moses for his divine destiny. His education would come from the Egyptians as he learned all about life near a Pharaoh. This would help him deal with a future Pharaoh as deliverer of God's people. Moses led sheep around a desert for forty years in preparation for another forty years leading God's sheep. Stephen's overview of Moses life continued.

> *23"When Moses was forty years old, he decided to visit his own people, the Israelites. 24He saw one of them being mistreated by an Egyptian, so he went to his defense and avenged him by killing the Egyptian. 25Moses thought that his own people would realize that God was using him to rescue them, but they did not. 26The next day Moses came upon two Israelites who were fighting. He tried to reconcile them by saying, 'Men,*

you are brothers; why do you want to hurt each other?'

27"But the man who was mistreating the other pushed Moses aside and said, 'Who made you ruler and judge over us? 28Are you thinking of killing me as you killed the Egyptian yesterday?' 29When Moses heard this, he fled to Midian, where he settled as a foreigner and had two sons.

30"After forty years had passed, an angel appeared to Moses in the flames of a burning bush in the desert near Mount Sinai. 31When he saw this, he was amazed at the sight. As he went over to get a closer look, he heard the Lord say: 32'I am the God of your fathers, the God of Abraham, Isaac and Jacob.' Moses trembled with fear and did not dare to look.

33"Then the Lord said to him, 'Take off your sandals, for the place where you are standing is holy ground. 34I have indeed seen the oppression of my people in Egypt. I have heard their groaning and have come down to set them free. Now come, I will send you back to Egypt.'

35"This is the same Moses they had rejected with the words, 'Who made you ruler and judge?' He was sent to

> be their ruler and deliverer by God himself, through the angel who appeared to him in the bush. 36He led them out of Egypt and performed wonders and signs in Egypt, at the Red Sea and for forty years in the wilderness. Acts 7:23-35

At the burning bush, the angel of the Lord called out to Moses. The four hundredth year of God's promise to set Abraham's ancestors free was approaching. Abraham's seed were crying out to God under their bondage of slavery. God prepares in advance for our destiny before it manifests in our lives. Earth had to be made ready for man before God formed Adam.

Moses thought his people would recognize him as a rescuer forty years earlier. *Moses thought* is the key here. He tried to do it on his own before God's timing and killed a man. The Lord called Moses by name, then began to direct his steps. There are set times on earth for God's plan to come to pass. At the burning bush, God made himself and his plan known to Moses. God then sent Moses to fulfill his destiny. In divine destiny, God will reveal his plan, but man must wait for God's command. Man must also come in agreement with God's plan for their lives once they understand it. Was Moses ready after all those years? Moses did not think so. Maybe Moses had given up on the notion to be a deliverer. After all it did not work out so well the first time, and 40 years had passed. Moses did not understand the big picture and probably thought he missed it until God made it clear to him. We will join the conversation between the Lord and Moses at the burning bush.

> *7The Lord said, "I have indeed seen the misery of my people in Egypt. I have heard them crying out because of their slave drivers, and I am concerned about their suffering. 8So I have come down to rescue them from the hand of the Egyptians and to bring them up out of that land into a good and spacious land, a land flowing with milk and honey—the home of the Canaanites, Hittites, Amorites, Perizzites, Hivites and Jebusites. 9And now the cry of the Israelites has reached me, and I have seen the way the Egyptians are oppressing them. 10So now, go. I am sending you to Pharaoh to bring my people the Israelites out of Egypt." Exodus 3:7-10*

The Word of the Lord to Moses explains the plight of the Israelites in Egypt. Within this Word contains a promise from God of what he intends to do. He states this in Exodus 3:8. Next he speaks to Moses, his chosen vessel through whom he will accomplish his promise. Then the command from God clearly reveals a step of action "Go." God's timing had come for Moses to fulfill his divine destiny. When? He was to get going right then.

> *11But Moses said to God, "Who am I that I should go to Pharaoh and bring the Israelites out of Egypt?"*

12And God said, "I will be with you. And this will be the sign to you that it is I who have sent you: When you have brought the people out of Egypt, you will worship God on this mountain."

13Moses said to God, "Suppose I go to the Israelites and say to them, 'The God of your fathers has sent me to you,' and they ask me, 'What is his name?' Then what shall I tell them?" 14God said to Moses, "I am who I am. This is what you are to say to the Israelites: 'I am has sent me to you.'"

15God also said to Moses, "Say to the Israelites, 'The Lord, the God of your fathers—the God of Abraham, the God of Isaac and the God of Jacob—has sent me to you.' "This is my name forever, the name you shall call me from generation to generation. 16"Go, assemble the elders of Israel and say to them, 'The Lord, the God of your fathers— the God of Abraham, Isaac and Jacob—appeared to me and said: I have watched over you and have seen what has been done to you in Egypt. 17And I have promised to bring you up out of your misery in Egypt into the land of the Canaanites, Hittites, Amorites,

Perizzites, Hivites and Jebusites—a land flowing with milk and honey'."

18"The elders of Israel will listen to you. Then you and the elders are to go to the king of Egypt and say to him, 'The Lord, the God of the Hebrews, has met with us. Let us take a three-day journey into the wilderness to offer sacrifices to the Lord our God.' 19But I know that the king of Egypt will not let you go unless a mighty hand compels him. 20So I will stretch out my hand and strike the Egyptians with all the wonders that I will perform among them. After that, he will let you go. 21"And I will make the Egyptians favorably disposed toward this people, so that when you leave you will not go empty-handed. 22Every woman is to ask her neighbor and any woman living in her house for articles of silver and gold and for clothing, which you will put on your sons and daughters. And so you will plunder the Egyptians." Exodus 3: 1122

1Moses answered, "What if they do not believe me or listen to me and say, 'The Lord did not appear to you'?" 2Then the Lord said to him, "What is that in your hand?" "A staff," he replied. 3The Lord said, "Throw it on the ground." Moses threw it on the ground and it became a snake, and he ran from it. 4Then the Lord said to him, "Reach out your hand and take it by the tail." So Moses reached out and took hold of the snake and it turned back into a staff in his hand. 5"This," said the Lord, "is so that they may believe that the Lord, the God of their fathers—the God of Abraham, the God of Isaac and the God of Jacob—has appeared to you." 6Then the Lord said, "Put your hand inside your cloak." So Moses put his hand into his cloak, and when he took it out, the skin was leprous —it had become as white as snow. 7"Now put it back into your cloak," he said. So Moses put his hand back into his cloak, and when he took it out, it was restored, like the rest of his flesh. 8Then the Lord said, "If they do not believe you or pay attention to the first sign, they may believe the second. 9But if they do not believe these two signs or listen to you, take some water from the Nile and pour it on the dry ground. The water you take from the river will become blood on the ground." 10Moses said to the Lord, "Pardon your servant, Lord. I have never been eloquent, neither in the past nor since you have spoken to your servant. I am slow of speech and tongue." 11The Lord said to him, "Who gave human beings their mouths? Who makes them deaf or mute? Who gives them sight or makes them blind? Is it not I, the Lord? 12Now go; I will help you speak and will teach you what to say." 13But Moses said, "Pardon your servant, Lord. Please send someone else."

14Then the Lord's anger burned against Moses and he said, "What about your brother, Aaron the Levite? I know he can speak well. He is already on his way to meet you, and he will be glad to see you. 15You shall speak to him and put words in his mouth; I will help both of you speak and will teach you what to do. 16He will speak to the people for you, and it will be as if he were your mouth and as if you were God to him. 17But take this staff in your hand so you can perform the signs with it." Exodus 4:1-14

For a man who killed an Egyptian as a deliverer of his people, Moses had come a long way. Not only did he make excuses, but he tried to get out of his divine destiny. God did not care for that response and was angry with Moses. God had used Moses' life to train him and get him ready. It was time for Israel to come out of Egypt. God was not going to take excuses from him. God assured Moses he would teach him and Aaron what to do and say. To fulfill divine destiny Moses must obey God's directive.

God gave Moses his first step to begin his destiny journey, *"So now, go. I am sending you to Pharaoh to bring my people the Israelites out of Egypt" (Exodus 3:10).* Moses had to believe what God told him before he could step out in faith. God knew how to get Moses' attention. Even though Moses was talking to God in a burning bush, our supernatural God doesn't stop there. God performs signs and wonders using Moses himself with the snake, leprosy, and the water turned into blood. Not only does Moses finally believe, these signs and wonders attest that indeed the God of Abraham, the God of Isaac, and the God of Jacob sent him. Moses demonstrates that he is finally ready to step out in his divine destiny. He goes home to prepare for his journey to Egypt. Not only did he prepare for his journey back to Egypt, he went. Simple and clear, he followed directions.

When God showed up at the burning bush, he did not tell Moses every part of his divine destiny. As God prepares a person to step out, he will provide the details needed to get moving. God knows the end from the beginning, but he is not going to tell us everything all up front.

> *I make known the end from the beginning, from ancient times, what is still to come. I say, 'My purpose will stand, and I will do all that I please.' Isaiah 46:10*

What if Moses knew that Israel would rebel against God once he led them out of Egypt? Or that he would lead them around a mountain for forty years as they died in the desert? What if he knew that only two men believed God to take possession of the Promised Land? If Moses knew all this ahead of time, he probably would have run the other way. God knows the big picture, but we get a piece at a time. Moses had a difficult time as the deliverer of Israel, but all was apart of his destiny. Even when a person fulfills divine destiny, it does not mean everything will be easy. God will not leave you or forsake you (Deuteronomy 31:6). Moses stuck it out and ran his race to receive the prize for which he was called.

Directives Given to Moses by God

To build faith in the reader that God will direct your path, I will list God's commands to Moses on his mission to deliver God's people from Egypt. Moses along with Aaron fulfilled these commands and completed their mission as God directed.

> *19Now the Lord had said to Moses in Midian, "Go back to Egypt, for all those who wanted to kill you are dead." Exodus 4:19*
>
> *21The Lord said to Moses, "When you return to Egypt, see that you perform before Pharaoh all the wonders I have given you the power to do. But I will harden his heart so that he will not let the people go. 22Then say to Pharaoh, 'This is what the Lord says: Israel is my firstborn son, 23and I told you, "Let my son go, so he may worship me." But you refused to let him go; so I will kill your firstborn son.'" Exodus 4:21-23*
>
> *27The Lord said to Aaron, "Go into the wilderness to meet Moses." So he met Moses at the mountain of God and kissed him. 28Then Moses told Aaron everything the Lord had sent him to say, and also about all the signs he had commanded him to perform. Exodus 4:27-28*

1Then the Lord said to Moses, "Now you will see what I will do to Pharaoh: Because of my mighty hand he will let them go; because of my mighty hand he will drive them out of his country." 2God also said to Moses, "I am the Lord. 3I appeared to Abraham, to Isaac and to Jacob as God Almighty, but by my name the Lord I did not make myself fully known to them. 4I also established my covenant with them to give them the land of Canaan, where they resided as foreigners. 5Moreover, I have heard the groaning of the Israelites, whom the Egyptians are enslaving, and I have remembered my covenant. Exodus 6:1-5

6"Therefore, say to the Israelites: 'I am the Lord, and I will bring you out from under the yoke of the Egyptians. I will free you from being slaves to them, and I will redeem you with an outstretched arm and with mighty acts of judgment. 7I will take you as my own people, and I will be your God. Then you will know that I am the Lord your God, who brought you out from under the yoke of the Egyptians. 8And I will bring you to the land I swore with uplifted hand to give to Abraham, to Isaac and to Jacob. I will give it to you as a possession. I am the Lord.'" 9Moses reported this to the Israelites, but they did not listen to him because of their discouragement and harsh labor. Exodus 6:6-9 10

Then the Lord said to Moses, 11"Go, tell Pharaoh king of Egypt to let the Israelites go out of his country." Exodus 6:10-11

13Now the Lord spoke to Moses and Aaron about the Israelites and Pharaoh king of Egypt, and he commanded them to bring the Israelites out of Egypt. Exodus 6:13

1Then the Lord said to Moses, "See, I have made you like God to Pharaoh, and your brother Aaron will be your prophet. 2You are to say everything I command you, and your brother Aaron is to tell Pharaoh to let the Israelites go out of his country. 3But I will harden Pharaoh's heart, and though I multiply my signs and wonders in Egypt, 4he will not listen to you. Then I will lay my hand on Egypt and with mighty acts of judgment I will bring out my divisions, my people the Israelites. 5And the Egyptians will know that I am the Lord when I stretch out my hand against Egypt and bring the Israelites out of it." 6Moses and Aaron did just as the Lord commanded them. 7Moses was eighty years old and Aaron eighty-three when they spoke to Pharaoh.

8The Lord said to Moses and Aaron, 9"When Pharaoh says to you, 'Perform a miracle,' then say to Aaron, 'Take your staff and throw it down before Pharaoh,' and it will become a snake." Exodus 7:1-9

14Then the Lord said to Moses, "Pharaoh's heart is unyielding; he refuses to let the people go. 15Go to Pharaoh in the morning as he goes out to the river. Confront him on the bank of the Nile, and take in your hand the staff that was changed into a snake. 16Then say to him, 'The Lord, the God of the Hebrews, has sent me to say to you: Let my people go, so that they may worship me in the wilderness. But until now you have not listened. 17This is what the Lord says: By this you will know that I am the Lord: With the staff that is in my hand I will strike the water of the Nile, and it will be changed into blood. 18The fish in the Nile will die, and the river will stink; the Egyptians will not be able to drink its water.'" Exodus 7:14-18

19The Lord said to Moses, "Tell Aaron, 'Take your staff and stretch out your hand over the waters of Egypt—over the streams and canals, over the ponds and all the reservoirs—and they will turn to blood.' Blood will be everywhere in

Egypt, even in vessels of wood and stone." 20Moses and Aaron did just as the Lord had commanded. Exodus 7:19-20

1Then the Lord said to Moses, "Go to Pharaoh and say to him, 'This is what the Lord says: Let my people go, so that they may worship me. 2If you refuse to let them go, I will send a plague of frogs on your whole country. Exodus 8:1-2

5Then the Lord said to Moses, "Tell Aaron, 'Stretch out your hand with your staff over the streams and canals and ponds, and make frogs come up on the land of Egypt.'" Exodus 8:5

Notice the details given to Moses by God in order to carry out his assignments. God promised, "I will help both of you speak and will teach you what to do" (Exodus 4:15b). He certainly did what he promised Moses, and he will do the same for you.

John the Baptist

Before I was born the LORD called me; from my mother's womb he has spoken my name. Isaiah 49:1

In the example of John the Baptist, I want the reader to see the foreknowledge of God before John's conception and birth. Hundreds of prophetic words were spoken of the coming Messiah as fulfilled in Jesus Christ, but for this brief study we will look at John's ministry.

Old Testament Foreknowledge of John

The prophet Isaiah spoke of the voice of one calling*"in the wilderness prepare the way for the Lord; make straight in the desert a highway for our God" (Isaiah 40:3).* John the Baptist fulfilled this prophetic declaration as confirmed in the New Testament. *"In those days John the Baptist came, preaching in the wilderness of Judea and saying, "Repent, for the kingdom of heaven has come near." This is he who was spoken of through the prophet Isaiah, "A voice of one calling in the wilderness, 'Prepare the way for the Lord, make straight paths for him'" (Matthew 3:1-3).*

Another prophet, Malachi foretold of John's calling as well. *"I will send my messenger, who will prepare the way before me. Then suddenly the Lord you are seeking will come to his temple; the messenger of the covenant, whom you desire, will come, says the Lord Almighty" (Malachi 3:1).*

New Testament Foreknowledge of John

Roughly four hundred years later, before John the Baptist was conceived, a word from the Lord was sent to a childless couple. The news was that they would soon be parents of a son named John. An angel sent from the Presence of God to Zechariah confirmed that his prayer for a son had been heard.

> *Then an angel of the Lord appeared to him, (Zechariah) standing at the right side of the altar of incense.12When Zechariah saw him, he was startled and was gripped with fear. 13But the angel said to him: "Do not be afraid, Zechariah; your prayer has been heard. Your wife Elizabeth will bear you a son, and you are to call him John. 14He will be a joy and delight to you, and many will rejoice because of his birth,15for he will be great in the sight of the Lord. He is never to take wine or other fermented drink, and he will be filled with the Holy Spirit even before he is born.*
>
> *18Zechariah asked the angel, "How can I be sure of this? I am an old man and my wife is well along in years." 19The angel said to him, "I am Gabriel. I stand in the presence of God, and I have been sent to speak to you and to tell you this good news. 20And now you will be*

silent and not able to speak until the day this happens, because you did not believe my words, which will come true at their appointed time." Luke 1:11-20

Zechariah was talking to an angel who spoke of a mighty fulfillment of his prayer. Zechariah's reaction was unbelief. He looked at their age and did not believe the angel's words which were set for an appointed time (Luke 1:20). God sent his word of divine destiny to Zachariah by the angel Gabriel. Just like with Moses, divine timing was at hand when God revealed the birth of John to Zachariah and Elizabeth. Zachariah's mouth of doubt and unbelief had to be silenced. Zechariah would return home to Elizabeth with the news. Zachariah could not talk, but he could write the angelic message telling Elizabeth she would conceive a son and his name would be John.

I bet Elizabeth grabbed the promise and did not let go. She had waited a long, long time. After Elizabeth conceived, she said. *"The Lord has done this for me. In these days he has shown his favor and taken away my disgrace among the people"* (Luke 1:20).

Zechariah and Elizabeth's news of a son came at a time set by God. John would be the one to prepare the way for the Lord. John's miracle conception came before another miracle conception that brought Jesus through Mary's womb. As the Messianic forerunner, six months after his conception this same angelic messenger was sent to Mary, the mother of Jesus. Her reaction to the angel's news was that she believed.

26In the sixth month of Elizabeth's pregnancy, God sent the angel Gabriel to Nazareth, a town in Galilee, 27to a virgin pledged to be married to a man named Joseph, a descendant of David. The virgin's name was Mary. 28The angel went to her and said, "Greetings, you who are highly favored! The Lord is with you." 29Mary was greatly troubled at his words and wondered what kind of greeting this might be. 30But the angel said to her, "Do not be afraid, Mary; you have found favor with God. 31You will conceive and give birth to a son, and you are to call him Jesus. 32He will be great and will be called the Son of the Most High. The Lord God will give him the throne of his father David, 33and he will reign over Jacob's descendants forever; his kingdom will never end." 34"How will this be," Mary asked the angel, "since I am a virgin?"

35The angel answered, "The Holy Spirit will come on you, and the power of the Most High will overshadow you. So the holy one to be born will be called the Son of God. 36Even Elizabeth your relative is going to have a child in her old age, and she who was said to be unable to conceive is in her sixth month. The Angel told Mary, 37For no word from God will ever fail." 38"I am the Lord's servant," Mary answered. "May your word to me be fulfilled." Then the angel left her.

The Holy Spirit accompanied the word released from the Presence of God by the angel Gabriel to perform it. God sent his angel to reveal divine destiny for Mary's life. Mary received the spoken word from the angel by faith. *Faith comes by hearing, hearing by the word of God (Romans 10:17).* Mary needed to be in an atmosphere of faith, so the angel included information on Elizabeth's miracle pregnancy. He did this to strengthened Mary's faith on the plan of God for her life. Mary ran to be near Elizabeth. God surely would perform his word for her as he did for Elizabeth. To fulfill divine destiny, place yourself around people who believe God and his word, that he still works by the power of the Holy Spirit today.

39At that time Mary got ready and hurried to a town in the hill country of Judea, 40where she entered Zechariah's home and greeted Elizabeth. 41When Elizabeth heard Mary's greeting, the baby leaped in her womb, and Elizabeth was filled with the Holy Spirit. 42In a loud voice she exclaimed: "Blessed are you among women, and blessed is the child you will bear! 43But why am I so favored, that the mother of my Lord should come to me? 44As soon as the sound of your greeting reached my ears, the baby in my womb leaped for joy. 45Blessed is

> *she who has believed that the Lord would fulfill his promises to her!" Luke 1:39-45*

At Mary's voice, Elizabeth, her baby, and Zachariah were all filled with the Holy Spirit. Then Elizabeth prophesied. Here again, we see the Holy Spirit at work to perform the word spoken by the angel to Zechariah. In the presence of the Lord, there is fullness of joy, even for an unborn baby. How awesome is our God who filled John with the Holy Spirit in his mother's womb.

> *You make known to me the path of life; you will fill me with joy in your presence, with eternal pleasures at your right hand. Psalms 16:11*

The God's foreknowledge of John shines forth once again. Filled with joy, Zechariah prophesied soon after his son's birth.

> *67His father Zechariah was filled with the Holy Spirit and prophesied:76And you, my child, will be called a prophet of the Most High; for you will go on before the Lord to prepare the way for him, 77to give his people the knowledge of salvation through the forgiveness of their sins, 78because of the tender mercy of our God, by which the rising sun will come to us from heaven 79to shine on those living in darkness and in the shadow of death, to guide our feet into the path of peace." 80And the child grew and*

> *became strong in spirit; and he lived in the wilderness until he appeared publicly to Israel. Luke 1:67:76-80*

Just as with Moses, the word of the Lord came to John to step out and do what God created him to do. Fulfillment comes to those who believe.

> *2during the high-priesthood of Annas and Caiaphas, the word of God came to John son of Zechariah in the wilderness. 3He went into all the country around the Jordan, preaching a baptism of repentance for the forgiveness of sins. Luke 3:2*

John was released to fulfill his divine destiny at this appointed time in history.

What did John do? He took the first step, the scripture says, "He went." That's all it took. His faith got him moving with just one step.

Baby Step 1

You Must Be Born Again

10For we are God's handiwork, created in Christ Jesus to do good works, which God prepared in advance for us to do. Ephesians 2:10 NIV

To get moving toward one's divine destiny, a relationship with the Lord must first be established. The one who knew you before being formed in your mother's womb is God, and he is the one who has the plans for your life. If you do not know the Lord or are not sure, then this is the first essential baby step.

Why We Must Be Born Again

The first man formed was Adam. God also made Adam a wife, and her name was Eve. Adam and Eve were free to enjoy God's creation with only one stipulation, a command from God that must be kept. Adam and Eve could eat from all but one tree located in the center of the garden. If Adam chose to disobey this one command, his life and the life of all mankind would be greatly altered.

> *16The LORD God commanded the man, saying, "From any tree of the garden you may eat freely; 17but from the tree of the knowledge of good and evil you shall not eat, for in the day that you eat from it you will surely die." Genesis 2:16-17 NIV*

Satan, a fallen angel, went to work to entice Adam and Eve to disobey this all important command. Notice it was just one command that Adam had to keep. Adam rebelled, and both he and Eve ate from the fruit growing on the forbidden tree. It was a decision made out of their soul that brought spiritual separation from God. This decision also brought physical death to all mankind. At the moment the fruit was eaten, there was an immediate spiritual separation of Adam and Eve from God. Prior to that event, Adam and his wife enjoyed an ongoing relationship with God. They were united to him by their spirits and were apart of the kingdom of God (Genesis, Chapters 1-3).

Therefore, just as sin entered the world through one man, and death through sin, and in this way death came to all people, because all sinned. Romans 5:12

Restoration Back To God

As God made man in his image, God did not want mankind separated from him, so he sought their restoration. He came up with a plan. God would send a second Adam, his own son, who would come in the likeness of sinful man. There would be one important distinction between the first Adam and the second. The second Adam would not fail, he would not rebel, and he would not sin. His name was Jesus, and he was tempted in every way as the first Adam. This plan of God put all punishment for the sins of all mankind on Jesus, the one who did not sin. Jesus would pay the penalty for us all by his body and bloodshed on the cross. After he died, his body was placed in a tomb. That's not the end of the story. On the third day after his death, the power of God resurrected Jesus from the dead.

> *For as in Adam all die, so in Christ all will be made alive. 1 Corinthians 15:22*

All humans are born with the same sin nature of Adam. As Adam was cut off from God due to his sin, all humans have this same problem. Jesus, the second Adam, made the way back for us to come into a relationship with God. "Salvation is found in no one else, for there is no other name under heaven given to mankind by which we must be saved" (Acts 4:12). Anyone who receives Jesus and his sacrificial death on the cross reaps a restored relationship with God.

> *So it is written: "The first man Adam became a living being"; the last Adam, a life-giving spirit. 1 Corinthians 15:45*

Jesus told a man named Nicodemus that no one would ever see the kingdom of God unless he or her were born again.

> *1Now there was a Pharisee, a man named Nicodemus who was a member of the Jewish ruling council. 2He came to Jesus at night and said, "Rabbi, we know that you are a teacher who has come from God. For no one could perform the signs you are doing if God were not with him." 3Jesus replied, "Very truly I tell you, no one can see the kingdom of God unless they are born again." John 3:1-3*

> *16For God so loved the world that he gave his one and only Son, that whoever believes in him shall not perish but have eternal life. 17For God did not send his Son into the world to condemn the world, but to save the world through him. 18Whoever believes in him is not condemned, but whoever does not believe stands condemned already because they have not believed in the name of God's one and only Son. John 3:1-3:16-18*

The Apostle Peter preached a message on the day of Pentecost which covers the steps that a person takes once he or she accepts the gift of salvation through Jesus Christ. We join him as he speaks.

> *"22"Fellow Israelites, listen to this: Jesus of Nazareth was a man accredited by God to you by miracles, wonders and signs, which God did among you through him, as you yourselves know. 23This man was handed over to you by God's deliberate plan and foreknowledge; and you, with the help of wicked men, put him to death by nailing him to the cross. 24But God raised him from the dead, freeing him from the agony of death, because it was impossible for death to keep its hold on him. 36"Therefore let all Israel be assured of this: God has made this Jesus, whom you crucified, both Lord and Messiah." 37When the people heard this, they were cut to the heart and said to Peter and the other apostles, "Brothers, what shall we do?" 38Peter replied, "Repent and be baptized, every one of you, in the name of Jesus Christ for the forgiveness of your sins. And you will receive the gift of the Holy Spirit. 39The promise is for you and your children and for all who are far off— for all whom the Lord our God will call." Acts 2:22-24:37-39*

By God's grace, his mercy, and his kindness, anyone can be saved from his or her sins. The requirement is to accept this free gift of salvation through Jesus Christ. Simply believe, and one will be saved by faith in the truth of this salvation message.

> *4 But because of his great love for us, God, who is rich in mercy, 5 made us alive with Christ even when we were dead in transgressions—it is by grace you have been saved. Ephesians 2:2-5 NIV*

After Jesus was resurrected, he came to his disciples and breathed the Holy Spirit upon them. Why did Jesus wait until after his resurrection?

> *19So when it was evening on that day, the first day of the week, and when the doors were shut where the disciples were, for fear of the Jews, Jesus came and stood in their midst and said to them, "Peace be with you." 20And when He had said this, He showed them both His hands and His side. The disciples then rejoiced when they saw the Lord. 21So Jesus said to them again, "Peace be with you; as the Father has sent Me, I also send you." 22And when He had said this, He breathed on them and said to them, "Receive the Holy Spirit. John 20:19-22*

When Jesus did this after his resurrection he established the New Covenant according to Romans 10:9-10.

> *"The word is near you; it is in your mouth and in your heart," that is, the message concerning faith that we proclaim: 9 If you declare with your mouth, Jesus is Lord," and believe in your heart that God raised him from the dead, you will be saved. 10 For it is with your heart that you believe and are justified, and it is with your mouth that you profess your faith and are saved. Romans 10:8b-10*

The disciples received the Holy Spirit as a deposit guaranteeing their inheritance in the kingdom of God.

> *And you also were included in Christ when you heard the message of truth, the gospel of your salvation. When you believed, you were marked in him with a seal, the promised Holy Spirit, 14who is a deposit guaranteeing our inheritance until the redemption of those who are God's possession—to the praise of his glory. Ephesians 1:13-14*

.

Baby Steps to be Born Again

For everyone has sinned; we all fall short of God's glorious standard. Romans 3:23 NLT

It does not take much for a child to lie. They do it easily. That is a sin. To repent means to be truly sorry for the wrong you personally have done. Repent also means to change. No one can do this without accepting Jesus and his payment for your sins. This first baby step is so important. Some people pray and ask for the new birth but do not truly repent of their sin. They are not sincere, so no real changes occur in their lives. The power of the cross will bring new birth, but it must be freely received as a gift from God, which comes out of God's mercy and grace.

And that message is the very message about faith that we preach: *9If you confess with your mouth that Jesus is Lord and believe in your heart that God raised him from the dead, you will be saved. 10For it is by believing in your heart that you are made right with God, and it is by confessing with your mouth that you are saved (Romans10: 9-10).*

.

> *"The time has come," he said. "The kingdom of God has come near. Repent and believe the good news!"*
> *Mark 1:15*

1. Repent and be truly sorry for your sins and change your mind from one of wrongdoing and turn to God.

2. Pray and tell God you are sorry for all your wrongdoing and then ask him to forgive you for it all.

3. Ask Jesus to come into your heart and for him to be your Lord and Savior. Jesus purchased you with his own life, and upon your repentance he saves you out of the kingdom of darkness and transfers you into the Kingdom of God. He is Lord and he becomes your master.

Baby Step

Prayer for Salvation

Here I am! I stand at the door and knock. If anyone hears my voice and opens the door, I will come in and eat with that person, and they with me. Rev 3:20

Lord, I realize that I am a sinner, and I make a decision right now to repent of my sins. I ask you to forgive me. I invite you, Lord Jesus, to come into my heart and be my Lord and Savior and to cleanse me of all unrighteousness. Because I ask, you are faithful and just to forgive me of my sins and place me into the Kingdom of God. Thank you for your mercy and this free gift of salvation through Jesus Christ.

Congratulations to all who have taken this first vital step to fulfilling your destiny.

Out of a born again spirit, the Holy Spirit will begin regeneration, to bring change in one's life that agrees with his word. For instance, if before you cursed, after new birth you will begin to realize that is something you do not want to continue. You will have the desire to stop. With the help of the Lord, you will begin to see these kinds of changes in your life.

One next becomes a disciple after repenting and accepting Christ's atonement for one's sins. A disciple is one taught of the Lord. How is a new believer taught of the Lord? Get around other disciples in a good Bible believing church, read your Bible, and develop a personal relationship with the Lord through your own prayer life.

> *Jesus came and told his disciples, "I have been given all authority in heaven and on earth. 19Therefore, go and make disciples of all the nations, baptizing them in the name of the Father and the Son and the Holy Spirit. 20Teach these new disciples to obey all the commands I have given you. And be sure of this: I am with you always, even to the end of the age." Matthew 28:18-19*

Baby Steps for Backsliders

Some people backslide. This means they have allowed themselves to ignore God and to live like they do not know him. This is a backslidden state. This is dangerous. In this state the kingdom of darkness is at work drawing a person away from the Lord. It becomes a critical matter living like this due to the hardening of your heart that may turn away from God. I implore you right now to stop and assess your life. Continuing to ignore the Holy Spirit's conviction or warning to stop what you're doing makes your heart hard. When your heart is hard, you do not yield to the Holy Spirit. The consequences of your sins come on you because you failed to stop.

I know of people that have gotten themselves in this state. Pain results as a consequence of their sin because of ignoring the conviction of the Holy Spirit.

If you are living like this and are tired of it, change your mind, repent, and turn back to God. Make a list of specific sins and prepare to pray. The Lord already knows, but you need to admit these for your sake.

.

Baby Step Prayer for a Backslider

Heavenly Father, I come to you, and I repent of everything (here you may list specific sins).)I do not want to live like this anymore. Thank you for listening to me. Now I ask you to forgive me for all my sin and wrongdoing. Have your way in my life. I need you and your help every day of my life. In the name of Jesus I pray. Amen.

.

Baby Step 2 - Water Baptism

After repentance of one's sins and acceptance of Jesus as Lord and Savior, the next step in a Christian's walk is to be water baptized. Water baptism is an outward sign that confirms a change in one's heart. This change can come only with the decision to accept Jesus Christ as Lord.

Jesus was water baptized by John the Baptist with full submersion in water. Through John's ministry water baptism was introduced for those who repented to receive forgiveness of their sins. He prepared the hearts of Israel for the coming Messiah.

> *4And so John the Baptist appeared in the wilderness, preaching a baptism of repentance for the forgiveness of sins." Mark 1:4*
>
> *29The next day John saw Jesus coming toward him and said, "Look, the Lamb of God, who takes away the sin of the world! 30This is the one I meant when I said, A man who comes after me has surpassed me because he was before me.' 31I myself did not know him, but the reason I came baptizing with water was that he might be revealed to Israel" John 1:29-31*

Jesus was not a sinner and he did not need to be baptized by John for the repentance of sins, and

John even declared it to him. The baptism of Jesus took place to fulfill all righteousness, and it demonstrated water baptism for Christian believers.

> *13Then Jesus came from Galilee to the Jordan to be baptized by John. 14But John tried to deter him, saying, "I need to be baptized by you, and do you come to me?" 15Jesus replied, "Let it be so now; it is proper for us to do this to fulfill all righteousness." Then John consented. Matthew 3:13-15*

The Trinity can be seen together in the water baptism of Jesus. God the Father, God the Son, and God the Holy Spirit were all present.

> *10Just as Jesus was coming up out of the water, he saw heaven being torn open and the Spirit descending on him like a dove. 11And a voice came from heaven: "You are my Son, whom I love; with you I am well pleased." Mark 1:10-11*

By this example of water baptism, Jesus told his disciples to baptize in the name of the Father, the Son, and of the Holy Spirit. The Trinity was at work at Jesus' baptism and will be with all believers.

> *18Then Jesus came to them and said, "All authority in heaven and on earth has been given to me. 19Therefore go and make disciples of all nations, baptizing them in the*

name of the Father and of the Son and of the Holy Spirit." Matthew 28:18-19 NIV

Baby Steps to Water Baptism

Or don't you know that all of us who were baptized into Christ Jesus were baptized into his death? 4We were therefore buried with him through baptism into death in order that, just as Christ was raised from the dead through the glory of the Father, we too may live a new life. Romans 6:3-4

Romans 6:4 brings to light the symbolism of the outward sign of water baptism. This represents death of the sinful man, then burial. When raised up from the water, it symbolizes resurrection from the dead through new birth. Water baptism identifies with Jesus death, burial, and resurrection from the dead.

Different Christian denominations have differing ways of water baptism. It is a matter of their preference and faith. I personally baptize in submerged water. Most churches have a baptismal which is filled with water for the service. The participants in water baptism will be those confessing Jesus as Lord and confirming their salvation with the outward sign of water baptism. In water baptism, one is quickly submerged under water holding one's nose and keeping their mouth shut. Just as John the Baptist baptized Jesus in water, there will be a minister leading the baptism service. Participants are baptized in the name of the Father, Son, and the Holy Spirit. When a baptismal is not available, a bathtub or a pool will do just fine.

Sometimes a person accepts Jesus as their Lord and Savior without a church home. In that case without delaying water baptism, go ahead and use a bathtub. If a Christian friend is available, that person can assist in the baptism service. I am not advocating not being apart of a local church, but when people receive salvation they do not want to delay water baptism, so don't. I have done more than one water baptism in a bathtub in order not to delay this outward sign of obedience to the word of God.

> *Then they that gladly received his word were baptized: and the same day there were added to them about three thousand soul. Acts 2:41*

My own water baptism was in a home bathtub. I was apart of a local church and had not arranged to be water baptized. On an out of town trip, a friend's church was having a baptism service. This church met in a rented room, so they did not have a baptismal. With the conviction of the Holy Spirit, I knew this was my opportunity, so I joined their service, and I am so glad I did.

> *18Then Jesus came to them and said, "All authority in heaven and on earth has been given to me. 19Therefore go and make disciples of all nations, baptizing them in the name of the Father and of the Son and of the Holy Spirit, 20and teaching them to obey everything I have commanded you. And surely I am with you always, to the very end of the age." Matthew 28:18 NIV*

Baby Steps to Water Baptism

1. Dress in clothes you do not mind getting wet.

2. Get into the water.

3.The minister conducting the service will specifically instruct you. For here, hold your nose with one hand, hold your breath, grab your arm with the other hand so the minister can assist you down and then quickly up from the water. You will be water baptized in the name of the Father, the Son, and the Holy Spirit. Catch your breath. You are now water baptized. Congratulations!.

The Holy Spirit Leads

For those who are led by the Spirit of God are the children of God. Romans 8:14

When new birth through Jesus Christ is received, how do you proceed toward divine destiny? When a person does not understand what to do in a given situation, help is needed.

I enjoy watching children gaze at the many delights on a lunch buffet we frequently enjoy. With eyes dancing from dish to dish, most older children have an idea of what they want to eat and go get it. Not so with the little ones. Without knowledge of the different foods, these tykes must rely on another. Generally, the small youngsters follow along as a mom or dad adds food to their plate. Parents know what they will eat and what not to give them. A watchful mom or dad also knows the dishes can be hot, so they ensure their child does not get burned. In eager anticipation, desserts and children share a natural magnet. A child's first stop can easily be for sweet treats with no thought of a single vegetable. So parents must provide the help their children need as well as oversight, guidance, and protection for an enjoyable lunch outing.

Our heavenly Father knows we also need help. It is the Holy Spirit who empowers believers to serve God. At the onset of Jesus' ministry, the Holy Spirit descended upon Jesus as the helper sent from God.

> *"But the Helper, the Holy Spirit, whom the Father will send in My name, He will teach you all things, and bring to your remembrance all that I said to you. John 14:26 NASB*

Without the Holy Spirit, Jesus would not have fulfilled his own calling and divine destiny. Right after the Holy Spirit came upon Jesus, the Holy Spirit began to lead him.

> *21Now when all the people were baptized, Jesus was also baptized, and while He was praying, heaven was opened, 22and the Holy Spirit descended upon Him in bodily form like a dove, and a voice came out of heaven, "You are My beloved Son, in You I am well-pleased." Luke 3:21-22 NIV*

Jesus was led by the Holy Spirit and informed by Him what was yet to come. Just as with Jesus, each believer must have the Holy Spirit at work in their lives to walk in their God given destiny.

> *Jesus, full of the Holy Spirit, left the Jordan and <u>was led by the Spirit</u> into the wilderness. Luke 4:1*

> *13But when he, the Spirit of truth, comes, he will guide you into all the truth. He will not speak on his own; he will speak only what he hears, and he will tell you what is yet to come. 14He will glorify me because it is from me that he will receive what*

he will make known to you. 15All that belongs to the Father is mine. That is why I said the Spirit will receive from me what he will make known to you." John 16:13-14 NIV

Jesus Walked in the Power of the Holy Spirit

14Jesus returned to Galilee in the power of the Spirit, and news about him spread through the whole countryside. 15He was teaching in their synagogues, and everyone praised him. Luke 4:14-15

Baptized in the Holy Spirit

The apostle Paul came across some disciples who had not received the Holy Spirit. After some questions Paul found these disciples were those of John the Baptist. They had not even heard of the Holy Spirit.

> *While Apollos was at Corinth, Paul took the road through the interior and arrived at Ephesus. There he found some disciples 2and asked them, "Did you receive the Holy Spirit when you believed?" They answered, "No, we have not even heard that there is a Holy Spirit." 3So Paul asked, "Then what baptism did you receive?" "John's baptism," they replied. 4Paul said, "John's baptism was a baptism of repentance. He told the people to believe in the one coming after him, that is, in Jesus." 5On hearing this, they were baptized in the name of the Lord Jesus. 6When Paul placed his hands on them, the Holy Spirit came on them, and they spoke in tongues and prophesied. 7There were about twelve men in all. Acts 19:1-6*

Once Paul explained the salvation message through Jesus Christ, they believed and then were water baptized. Paul did not stop there, next he laid his hands on them to receive the Holy Spirit. The evidence they received the Holy Spirit was that they spoke in tongues and prophesied.

The proof of the baptism in the Holy Spirit will be speaking in tongues. Those filled with the Holy Spirit may also praise God and prophesy. After Peter preached on the day of Pentecost, all who believed were filled with the Holy Spirit and spoke in tongues.

> *All of them were filled with the Holy Spirit and began to speak in other tongues as the Spirit enabled them. Acts 2:4*
>
> *44While Peter was still speaking these words, the Holy Spirit came on all who heard the message. 45The circumcised believers who had come with Peter were astonished that the gift of the Holy Spirit had been poured out even on Gentiles. 46For they heard them speaking in tongues and praising God. Acts10:44-45*
>
> *And these signs will accompany those who believe: In my name they will drive out demons; they will speak in new tongues; Mark16:17*
>
> *Paul said he spoke in tongues more than any other believer at the church in Corinth. "I thank God that I speak*

in tongues more than all of you" (1 Corinthians 14:18).

In my life, I was saved, baptized in the Holy Spirit, and then water baptized. How did this happen in this order? God is so merciful. I needed his help, and he got me where I would receive prayer to be filled with the Holy Spirit. My prayer language of speaking in tongues came at a church service before I had the chance to be water baptized. I did not know how to pray for my situation and receiving my prayer language took care of that. I just needed to pray in tongues, and I knew God's will would come about.

> *26In the same way, the Spirit helps us in our weakness. We do not know what we ought to pray for, but the Spirit himself intercedes for us through wordless groans. 27And he who searches our hearts knows the mind of the Spirit, because the Spirit intercedes for God's people in accordance with the will of God. Romans 8:26-27*

Jesus needed to be baptized in the Holy Spirit and promised his disciples the same gift. "*On one occasion, while he was eating with them, he gave them this command: 'Do not leave Jerusalem, but wait for the gift my Father promised, which you have heard me speak about. For John baptized with water, but in a few days you will be baptized with the Holy Spirit' " (Acts 1:4-5).*

> *3After his suffering, he presented himself to them and gave many*

convincing proofs that he was alive. He appeared to them over a period of forty days and spoke about the kingdom of God. 4On one occasion, while he was eating with them, he gave them this command: "Do not leave Jerusalem, but wait for the gift my Father promised, which you have heard me speak about. 5For John baptized with water, but in a few days you will be baptized with the Holy Spirit." Acts 1:3-5

If Jesus, the apostles, his disciples, and new believers received the baptism in the Holy Spirit in the New Testament, so can believers in Christ Jesus today.

.

Baby Step 3

Be Filled with the Holy Spirit

Anything one receives from God will be by faith. The baptism in the Holy Spirit comes the same way. Simply believe. In the same way one receives salvation, one receives the Baptism in the Holy Spirit. When you pray and ask to be baptized with the Holy Spirit, that is what you will receive. The gifts of God are without repentance. This means once you ask God for the gift of the Holy Spirit with the evidence of speaking in tongues, then this gift will not be taken from you.

> *For the gifts and calling of God are without repentance. Romans 11:29 KJ*

> *9"So I say to you: Ask and it will be given to you; seek and you will find; knock and the door will be opened to you. 10For everyone who asks receives; the one who seeks finds; and to the one who knocks, the door will be opened. 11"Which of you fathers, if your son asks for a fish, will give him a snake instead? 12Or if he asks for an egg, will give him a scorpion? 13If you then, though you are evil, know how to give good gifts to your children, how much more will your Father in heaven give the Holy Spirit to those who ask him!" Luke 11:9-12*

Prayer for the
Baptism in the Holy Spirit

1. Come to the Lord in prayer with a clean conscious. Repent of any sin in your life.

2. Pray and ask the Lord to baptize you with the Holy Spirit and enable you to speak in tongues.

3. Pray in tongues. Now open your mouth to speak and allow the Holy Spirit to give you words you do not understand. It will sound funny to you at first, but keep going. Pray and allow the different tongues to come forth.

I had so much prayer need in the beginning of receiving the Baptism in the Holy Spirit that I felt like a dam just broke. I felt so refreshed. Keep praying and know the will of God shall come to pass as you pray in tongues.

Prayer for the Baptism in the Holy Spirit.

Heavenly Father, thank you for forging me and for salvation through Jesus my Lord and Savior. I now ask that you fill me with the Holy Spirit. I understand the evidence of the baptism in the Holy Spirit is speaking in tongues. Thank you for hearing and answering my prayer and filling me with the Holy Spirit, in the name of Jesus I pray.

The Essentials for a Christian

1. Prayer is a must in a relationship with God. Prayer simply is communication with Him. It may consist of asking Him for help in whatever situation of your life and thanking Him for all does. Jesus taught his disciples how to pray.

> 9 "This, then, is how you should pray: " ' Our Father in heaven, hallowed be your name, 10 your kingdom come, your will be done on earth as it is in heaven. 11 Give us today our daily bread. 12 Forgive us our debts, as we also have forgiven our debtors. 13 And lead us not into temptation, but deliver us from the evil one'." Matthew 6:9-15

2. Pray in tongues daily. Scripture tells us to pray in our understanding and in tongues. I make sure I pray in tongues everyday which brings God's will into the situation of my prayers.

> 4For if I pray in a tongue, my spirit prays, but my mind is unfruitful. 15So what shall I do? I will pray with my spirit, but I will also pray with my understanding... 1 Corinthians 14:14

3. Praise and worship the Lord. This comes out of a heart gratitude and thankfulness for all God He is and does.

4. Allow the Holy Spirit to lead. He leads every member of the Body of Christ according to the word

and the will of God. Each step a person takes led by the Holy Spirit works together to bring about divine purpose in one's life.

5. Know the word of God. How? Read the Bible and mediate on it. Let the scriptures rule in your life by becoming a doer of the word. As the Word of God becomes stored in your heart, the Holy Spirit can bring what you've learned back to your memory.

> *Do not merely listen to the word, and so deceive yourselves. Do what it says. James 1:22*
>
> *26But the Advocate, the Holy Spirit, whom the Father will send in my name, will teach you all things and will remind you of everything I have said to you. John 14:26*

6. Find a good Bible believing church where you can grow as a disciple of the Lord Jesus Christ. Then go and be apart of what the Lord is doing there. The Holy Spirit will lead you to the best match for you in a church home.

Steps of Action

To walk in divine destiny, there are steps of action in the process. These are the same as the essentials, but I will show you how to apply them to achieve your destiny.

An example is writing a book. The Holy Spirit places a topic on my heart, so that's where I begin. To achieve the Lord's purpose I pray. I ask for his will to take place in my life and in the book I am writing. As I continue to pray in tongues over the project, the topic expands in different aspects. Next I form an outline. When I get an outline, that is where I begin. Most of the time I am not sure exactly how a book will actually flow. The outline gets me in faith and a place to begin. The Holy Spirit will lead and guide me in the way I should go in a book, so he leads and I follow. This continues throughout the whole process. Even when I think I am done, I pray until I am released in my spirit concerning the book. I will have peace and know I am at a stopping point.

This is how a walk with God works. Out of a lifestyle of prayer and obedience to the leading of the Holy Spirit, fulfillment comes. Much joy arises from a thankful heart as one witnesses the Lord perform his word. Year after year, situation after situation, faith after faith, the Lord is faithful. Then after a while, one can look back and see all the Lord accomplished through your life.

By following the essentials, continue to walk in a relationship with the Lord. Have an active prayer life as well as worship of God. He will show you the way to go. Pay attention to the Holy Spirit. This will save you a lot of time, money and heartache. A walk with God takes a lifetime. As one walks it out, fulfillment of your divine destiny takes place.

God knows the hearts of those who will fulfill different purposes for him. Many do not know of their divine purpose because they do not walk with the Lord. In such a case, God must capture their attention to move them close to him. With Moses, it took the burning bush. Once Moses came near, then God could direct his steps to fulfill the divine plan for his life. If this applies to the reader, draw near to God, and he will draw near to you.

> *Draw near to God, and he will draw near to you. Cleanse your hands, you sinners, and purify your hearts, you double-minded. James 4:8*

Baby Steps of Action

1. Walk in the essentials as a regular part of your life.

2. As you pray, seek God's will for your life and any specific situation.

3. Pray in tongues and the Holy Spirit will direct your paths.

4. When steps of action are placed on one's heart by the Holy Spirit, take the first baby step in obedience and keep going. Remember, God promised to teach Moses and Aaron what to say as they went along. He did not expect them to know everything in the beginning. God just needed Moses to go, and then he could direct his steps.

Just Do It - Take a Baby Step

I want the reader to know you are important. God has a plan and divine purpose just for you. Without you, it could not come about. God knows the number of hairs on your head, so believe it.

> *And even the very hairs of your head are all numbered. Matthew 10:30*

If one knows he or she is called to a certain profession, just wanting this does not make it happen. Steps of action must be discovered to bring it about in one's life. As a Christian, rely on the Lord to lead you in the way you should go. In so doing, the path will be made clear before you. What happens if there are more than one way to go or if confusion arises? God is not the master of confusion. If there is no peace, then don't do it. Wait. The kingdom of darkness is behind confusion and fear. These are designed to stop faith in God's will coming to pass.

> *And no wonder, for Satan himself masquerades as an angel of light. 1 Corinthians 1:14*

Do your research and find out the information required to make sound decisions. The Holy Spirit leads you in peace, so if you do not have peace wait until you are clear on the direction to take.

> *You will go out in joy and be led forth in peace…Isaiah 55:12*

It takes one step at a time to accomplish any goal. A walk led by the Spirit of God requires you to listen to the steps the Holy Spirit places in your heart to do. He knows where you are and where you need to go. Be patient and if you mess up, get up and keep going in the way you should go.

> *"And the LORD will continually guide you . ". . Isaiah 58:11 NASB*

A while back in a church service, some people were struggling to make progress in their walk with God. A word of encouragement came: take just one small step forward. After the first small step, the Lord would reveal the next one. With one baby step leading to another, one would finally be walking in the way they should go. Instead of struggling, a forward movement to destiny could be obtained by one baby step at a time. Stepping out on just one command brought faith.

As one keeps going, divine destiny is being fulfilled in your life. Now it's the readers turn to get moving, one baby step at a time.

My Prayer for Those Who Read This Book and Desire to be Used of God.

Heavenly Father, Just as Moses stepped out and did what you called him to do. I pray that the readers of this book step out to fulfill their divine destinies. I ask that you clearly direct their steps in your perfect timing. I pray that this little book go around the world and touch those who want to serve the Living God. For your Glory, In Jesus name I pray.

Contact the Author

Vickie Bryan

vickiebryan.com

endtimenephilim.com

V Ly Publishing LLC
Christian Imprint Books
1046 Church Rd, W 106-224
Southaven, MS 38671

Other Books by Vickie Bryan

Living with the Nephilim
the Seed of Destruction

Adolf Hitler Origins of a Psychopath

www.ingramcontent.com/pod-product-compliance
Lightning Source LLC
Chambersburg PA
CBHW071315110426
42743CB00042B/2430